Kansas Ecoregions

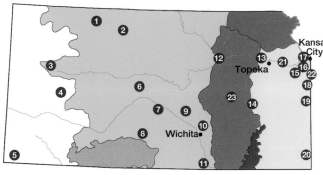

- ☐ High Plains
- ☐ Central Great Plains
- ☐ Southwestern Tablelands
- ☐ Western Corn Belt Plains
- ☐ Flint Hills
- ☐ Central Irregular Plains
- ☐ Cross Timbers

1. Prairie Dog State Park
2. Kirwin National Wildlife Refuge (NWR)
3. Scott State Park
4. Sandsage Bison Range Wildlife Area
5. Cimarron National Grassland
6. Kansas Wetlands Education Center
7. Quivira NWR
8. Pratt Education Center
9. Dillon Nature Center
10. Great Plains Nature Center
11. Chaplin Nature Center
12. Milford Nature Center
13. W. Clement Stone Nature Center
14. Flint Hills NWR
15. Olathe Prairie Center
16. Ernie Miller Nature Center
17. Mr. & Mrs. F.L. Schlagle Environmental Library
18. Prairie Oak Nature Center
19. Marais Des Cygnes NWR
20. Southeast Kansas Nature Center
21. University of Kansas Natural History Museum
22. Museum at Prairiefire
23. Schmidt Museum of Natural History

KANSAS WILDLIFE – A Folding Pocket Guide to Familiar Animals

KANSAS WILDLIFE

A Folding Pocket Guide to Familiar Animals

WATERFORD PRESS

Giant Redheaded Centipede
Scolopendra heros
To 10 in. (25 cm)

Fire Ant
Solenopsis geminata
To .25 in. (.6 cm)
Named for its painful, burning sting.

Migratory Grasshopper
Melanoplus sanguinipes
To 1.5 in. (4 cm)

Fiddleback Spider (Brown Recluse Spider)
Loxosceles reclusa
To .5 in. (1.5 cm)
Easily distinguished by the violin-shaped marking on its back. Bites cause tissue degeneration.

Wolf Spider
Family Lycosidae
To 1.5 in. (4 cm)
Most do not weave webs but catch prey by pouncing on it.

Black-and-yellow Garden Spider
Argiope aurantia
To 1.25 in. (3.2 cm)

Bumble Bee
Bombus spp.
To 1 in. (3 cm)
Stout, furry bee is large and noisy. Can sting repeatedly.

Honey Bee
Apis mellifera
To .75 in. (2 cm)
Slender bee has pollen baskets on its rear legs. Can only sting once. **Kansas's state insect.**

Yellow Jacket
Vespula pensylvanica
To .63 in. (1.6 cm)
Aggressive picnic pest can sting repeatedly.

Tiger Beetle
Family Cicindelidae
To 1 in. (3 cm)
Active beetle has long legs, large eyes and prominent jaws. Back is often spotted.

Backswimmer
Family Notonectidae
To .5 in. (1.3 cm)
Swims on back and often rests at or just below the surface.

American Cockroach
Periplaneta americana
To 2 in. (5 cm)

Water Strider
Gerris spp. To .5 in. (1.3 cm)
Long-legged insect skates along the surface of the water.

Water Boatman
Family Corixidae
To .5 in. (1.3 cm)
Swims erratically.

Whirligig Beetle
Gyrinus spp.
To .5 in. (1.3 cm)
Large swarms swirl around on the water's surface.

Black Swallowtail
Papilio polyxenes
To 3.5 in. (9 cm)

Eastern Tiger Swallowtail
Papilio glaucus
To 6 in. (15 cm)

Pipevine Swallowtail
Battus philenor
To 3.5 in. (9 cm)

Monarch
Danaus plexippus
To 4 in. (10 cm)

Cabbage White
Pieris rapae
To 2 in. (5 cm)
One of the most common butterflies.

Orange Sulphur
Colias eurytheme
To 2.5 in. (6 cm)
Gold-orange butterfly has a prominent forewing spot.

Viceroy
Limenitis archippus
To 3 in. (8 cm)
Told from similar monarch by its smaller size and the thin, black band on its hindwings.

Gray Hairstreak
Strymon melinus
To 1.25 in. (3.2 cm)
Note orange spots on hindwings. Underwings are blue-gray.

Eastern Tailed Blue
Cupido comyntas
To 1 in. (3 cm)
Note orange spots above thread-like hindwing tails.

Spring Azure
Celastrina ladon
To 1.3 in. (3.6 cm)
One of the earliest spring butterflies.

American Snout
Libytheana carinenta
To 2 in. (5 cm)
"Snout" is formed from projecting mouth parts which enclose its coiled "nose."

Pearly Crescentspot
Phyciodes tharos
To 1.5 in. (4 cm)
Hindwing is marked with dark crescent-shaped spots.

Common Wood-Nymph
Cercyonis pegala nephele
To 3 in. (8 cm)
Note 2 "eyespots" on the forewing.

Mourning Cloak
Nymphalis antiopa
To 3.5 in. (9 cm)
Emerges during the first spring thaw.

Red Admiral
Vanessa atalanta
To 2.5 in. (6 cm)

Rainbow Trout
Oncorhynchus mykiss To 44 in. (1.1 m)
Note reddish side stripe.

Largemouth Bass
Micropterus salmoides To 40 in. (1 m)
Note prominent stripe down side, jaw extends past eye.

Striped Bass
Morone saxatilis To 6 ft. (1.8 m)
Has 6-9 dark side stripes.

Smallmouth Bass
Micropterus dolomieu To 27 in. (68 cm)
Jaw joint is beneath the eye.

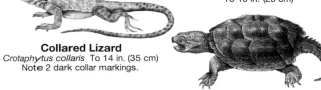

White Bass
Morone chrysops To 18 in. (45 cm)
Silvery fish has 4-7 dark side stripes.

Wiper
Morone hybrid To 20 in. (50 cm)
Note broken side stripes. Striped and white bass hybrid may be tho most aggressive Kansas sport fish.

Crappie
Pomoxis spp.
To 20 in. (50 cm)

Redear Sunfish
Lepomis microlophus To 14 in. (35 cm)

Green Sunfish
Lepomis cyanellus
To 12 in. (30 cm)

Bluegill
Lepomis macrochirus To 16 in. (40 cm)

Walleye
Sander vitreum To 40 in. (1 m)

Sauger
Sander canadense To 30 in. (75 cm)
Note dark "saddles" on back.

Channel Catfish
Ictalurus punctatus To 4 ft. (1.2 m)
Note adipose fin, black-spotted sides and rounded anal fin. **Kansas's state fish.**

Flathead Catfish
Pylodictis olivaris To 5 ft. (1.5 m)
Head is long and flat.

Gray Treefrog
Hyla versicolor
To 2.5 in. (6 cm)
Call is a strong, resonating trill.

Northern Leopard Frog
Lithobates pipiens
To 4 in. (10 cm)
Brown to green frog has dark spots on its back. Call is a rattling snore with grunts and moans.

Great Plains Toad
Anaxyrus cognatus
To 4 in. (10 cm)
Call is a metallic trill.

Barred Tiger Salamander
Ambystoma tigrinum mavortium
To 9 in. (23 cm)
Kansas's state amphibian.

Ornate Box Turtle
Terrapene ornata
To 5 in. (13 cm)
Kansas's state reptile.

Five-lined Skink
Plestiodon fasciatus To 8 in. (20 cm)
Has 5 light dorsal stripes.

Painted Turtle
Chrysemys picta
To 10 in. (25 cm)

Collared Lizard
Crotaphytus collaris To 14 in. (35 cm)
Note 2 dark collar markings.

Snapping Turtle
Chelydra serpentina To 18 in. (45 cm)
Note knobby shell and long tail.

Western Hognose Snake
Heterodon nasicus To 3 ft. (90 cm)
Thick snake has an upturned snout. Color varies.

Red-sided Garter Snake
Thamnophis sirtalis parietalis
To 4 ft. (1.2 m)

Northern Water Snake
Nerodia sipedon To 4.5 ft. (1.4 m)
Note dark blotches on back.

Prairie Rattlesnake
Crotalus viridis viridis
To 5 ft. (1.5 m)
Venomous snake has a spade-shaped head. W. Kansas.

Corn Snake
Pantherophis guttatus To 6 ft. (1.8 m)
Told by black-bordered, red blotches.

Canada Goose
Branta canadensis
To 45 in. (1.14 m)

Snow Goose
Chen caerulescens
To 31 in. (78 cm)

Trumpeter Swan
Cygnus buccinator
To 6 ft. (1.8 m)
Note stout black bill.

Mallard
Anas platyrhynchos To 28 in. (70 cm)

American Wigeon
Mareca americana
To 23 in. (58 cm)

Wood Duck
Aix sponsa To 20 in. (50 cm)

Northern Pintail
Anas acuta To 30 in. (75 cm)

Green-winged Teal
Anas crecca To 15 in. (38 cm)

Blue-winged Teal
Spatula discors To 16 in. (40 cm)

American Avocet
Recurvirostra americana
To 20 in. (50 cm)

Ruby-throated Hummingbird
Archilochus colubris
To 3.5 in. (9 cm)

Great Blue Heron
Ardea herodias
To 4.5 ft. (1.4 m)

Great Egret
Ardea alba
To 38 in. (95 cm)
Note yellow bill and black feet.

Greater Prairie-Chicken
Tympanuchus cupido
To 18 in. (45 cm)

Wild Turkey
Meleagris gallopavo
To 4 ft. (1.2 m)

Yellow-billed Cuckoo
Coccyzus americanus
To 14 in. (35 cm)

Ring-necked Pheasant
Phasianus colchicus
To 3 ft. (90 cm)

American Kestrel
Falco sparverius
To 12 in. (30 cm)

Mourning Dove
Zenaida macroura
To 13 in. (33 cm)
Call is a mournful –
ooah-woo-woo-woo.

Turkey Vulture
Cathartes aura
To 32 in. (80 cm)
Note red head and
two-toned underwings.

Red-tailed Hawk
Buteo jamaicensis
To 25 in. (63 cm)

Bald Eagle
Haliaeetus leucocephalus
To 40 in. (1 m)

Great Horned Owl
Bubo virginianus
To 25 in. (63 cm)
Call is a resonant –
hoo-HOO-hoooo.

Red-headed Woodpecker
Melanerpes erythrocephalus
To 10 in. (25 cm)

Northern Flicker
Colaptes auratus
To 13 in. (33 cm)
Wing and tail
linings are yellow.

Downy Woodpecker
Dryobates pubescens
To 6 in. (15 cm)
The similar hairy
woodpecker is larger
and has a longer bill.

Barred Owl
Strix varia
To 2 ft. (60 cm)
Call is a loud –
who-cooks-for-you?
who-cooks-for-
you-all?

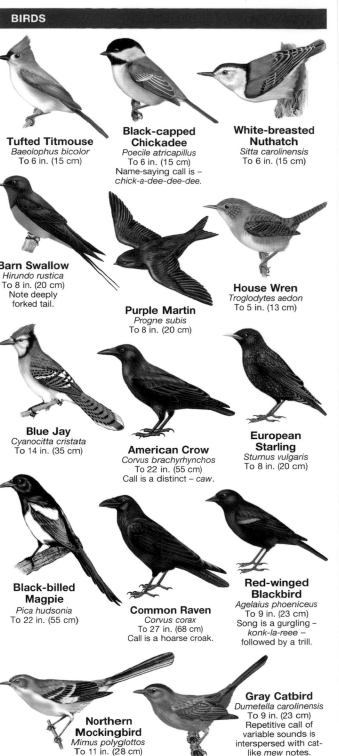

Tufted Titmouse
Baeolophus bicolor
To 6 in. (15 cm)

Black-capped Chickadee
Poecile atricapillus
To 6 in. (15 cm)
Name-saying call is –
chick-a-dee-dee-dee.

White-breasted Nuthatch
Sitta carolinensis
To 6 in. (15 cm)

Barn Swallow
Hirundo rustica
To 8 in. (20 cm)
Note deeply
forked tail.

Purple Martin
Progne subis
To 8 in. (20 cm)

House Wren
Troglodytes aedon
To 5 in. (13 cm)

Blue Jay
Cyanocitta cristata
To 14 in. (35 cm)

American Crow
Corvus brachyrhynchos
To 22 in. (55 cm)
Call is a distinct – caw.

European Starling
Sturnus vulgaris
To 8 in. (20 cm)

Black-billed Magpie
Pica hudsonia
To 22 in. (55 cm)

Common Raven
Corvus corax
To 27 in. (68 cm)
Call is a hoarse croak.

Red-winged Blackbird
Agelaius phoeniceus
To 9 in. (23 cm)
Song is a gurgling –
konk-la-reee –
followed by a trill.

Northern Mockingbird
Mimus polyglottos
To 11 in. (28 cm)

Gray Catbird
Dumetella carolinensis
To 9 in. (23 cm)
Repetitive call of
variable sounds is
interspersed with cat-
like mew notes.

Eastern Bluebird
Sialia sialis
To 7 in. (18 cm)

American Robin
Turdus migratorius
To 11 in. (28 cm)

Horned Lark
Eremophila alpestris
To 8 in. (20 cm)

Baltimore Oriole
Icterus galbula
To 8 in. (20 cm)

Dickcissel
Spiza americana
To 7 in. (18 cm)

Western Meadowlark
Sturnella neglecta
To 9 in. (23 cm)
Kansas's state bird.

Yellow Warbler
Setophaga petechia
To 5 in. (13 cm)

Cedar Waxwing
Bombycilla cedrorum
To 7 in. (18 cm)
Red wing marks look
like waxy droplets.

Pine Siskin
Spinus pinus
To 5 in. (13 cm)

Indigo Bunting
Passerina cyanea
To 6 in. (15 cm)

House Sparrow
Passer domesticus
To 6 in. (15 cm)

House Finch
Haemorhous mexicanus
To 6 in. (15 cm)

Northern Cardinal
Cardinalis cardinalis
To 9 in. (23 cm)

American Goldfinch
Spinus tristis
To 5 in. (13 cm)

Dark-eyed Junco
Junco hyemalis
To 7 in. (18 cm)

Black-tailed Jackrabbit
Lepus californicus To 25 in. (63 cm)
Tail and ears are black-tipped.

Eastern Cottontail
Sylvilagus floridanus
To 18 in. (45 cm)

Big Brown Bat
Eptesicus fuscus
To 5 in. (13 cm)

House Mouse
Mus musculus
To 8 in. (20 cm)
Introduced pest
has a naked tail.

Norway Rat
Rattus norvegicus
To 18 in. (45 cm)
Brown to gray rodent
has a naked tail.

Deer Mouse
Peromyscus maniculatus
To 8 in. (20 cm)
Distinguished by its white
undersides and hairy tail.

Thirteen-lined Ground Squirrel
Spermophilus tridecemlineatus
To 12 in. (30 cm)

Eastern Gray Squirrel
Sciurus carolinensis
To 20 in. (50 cm)

Fox Squirrel
Sciurus niger
To 28 in. (70 cm)
Note large size and
bushy tail. Coat may
be dark gray, red-
brown or black.

Virginia Opossum
Didelphis virginiana
To 40 in. (1 m)

Black-tailed Prairie Dog
Cynomys ludovicianus
To 16 in. (40 cm)
Tail is black-tipped.

Woodchuck
Marmota monax
To 32 in. (80 cm)

Common Muskrat
Ondatra zibethicus
To 2 ft. (60 cm)
Aquatic rodent has a naked tail
that is flattened on its sides.

Nine-banded Armadillo
Dasypus novemcinctus
To 32 in. (80 cm)

American Badger
Taxidea taxus
To 35 in. (88 cm)

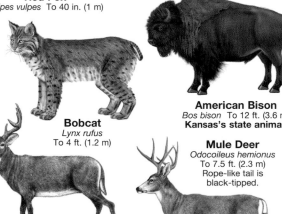

Common Porcupine
Erethizon dorsatum To 3 ft. (90 cm)

Striped Skunk
Mephitis mephitis
To 32 in. (80 cm)

Common Raccoon
Procyon lotor To 40 in. (1 m)

American Beaver
Castor canadensis
To 4 ft. (1.2 m)

Common Gray Fox
Urocyon cinereoargenteus
To 3.5 ft. (1.1 m)

Coyote
Canis latrans To 52 in. (1.3 m)

Kit Fox
Vulpes macrotis
To 34 in. (85 cm)

Red Fox
Vulpes vulpes To 40 in. (1 m)

Bobcat
Lynx rufus
To 4 ft. (1.2 m)

American Bison
Bos bison To 12 ft. (3.6 m)
Kansas's state animal.

Mule Deer
Odocoileus hemionus
To 7.5 ft. (2.3 m)
Rope-like tail is
black-tipped.

White-tailed Deer
Odocoileus virginianus
To 7 ft. (2.1 m)
Fluffy tail is white below.